Canadian Rockies ABC

For Darmody and Mac O'Donnell, who constantly remind me to play

CANADIAN ROCKIES ABC

Published by

Summerthought

Summerthought Publishing
PO Box 2309
Banff, AB T1L 1C1
Canada
www.summerthought.com

1st Edition—2010

Text and illustrations copyright © 2010 by Max Elliott

Production: Linda Petras
Printed in Canada by Friesens

We gratefully acknowledge the financial support of the Alberta Foundation for the Arts for our publishing activities.

Library and Archives Canada Cataloguing in Publication

Elliott, Max, 1962-
    Canadian Rockies ABC / Max Elliott.

ISBN 978-0-9811491-4-1

1. English language—Alphabet—Juvenile literature. 2. Rocky Mountains, Canadian (B.C. and Alta.)—Pictorial works—Juvenile literature. 3. Alphabet books. I. Title.

PE1155.E44 2010   j421'.1   C2009-907129-0

Canadian Rockies ABC

by Max Elliott

Bb is for bear
sound asleep in the sun

Cc is for camping
by lakes
deep and clear

Dd is for doe, a mama deer

Ee is for elk
with his antlers
held high

Hh is for hiking
to a great height

I i is for ice-skating
– Hey, look at me!

Jj is for jay
singing joyfully

Kk is for kayaking
quickly downstream

Mm is for moose
just wandering by

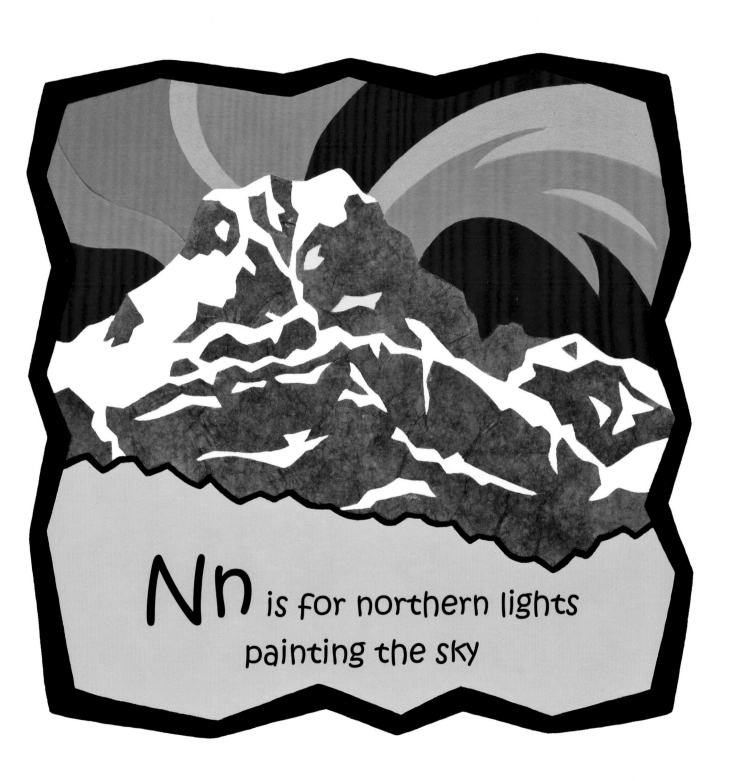

Nn is for northern lights
painting the sky

Oo is for owl
high in a tree

Qq is for quills
of a porcupine

Ss is for snowflakes
and snowman and skis

Tt is for train through tunnels and trees

Vv is for valley
and a wonderful view

Ww is for
waterfall
splashing our
faces

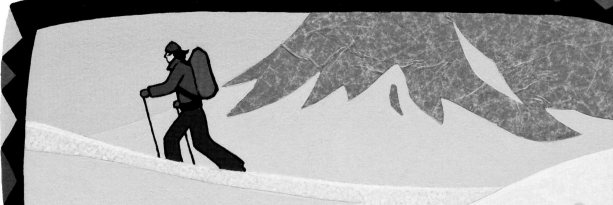

Xx is for X-country skiing to beautiful places

Yy is for yes!
to more
mountain fun

Growing up in the Canadian Rockies is a unique and special experience, with year-round adventures for all ages. As these quotes from local children show, each season brings with it new joys and exciting adventures.

Taking my wildflower book on nature walks
— Molly (4), Canmore

Fishing with my dad
— Skylar (5), Jasper

Riding my mountain bike along bumpy trails
— Finn (6), Banff

Skiing black diamond runs without my parents
— James (8), Lake Louise

Roasting marshmallows around a campfire
— Al (7), Banff

Playing on the beach and splashing in the cold water
— Griffin (3), Jasper

Riding the gondola with my friends
— Emma (4), Golden

Skating outdoors on frozen lakes
— Brio (5), Banff

Looking for pikas in rock piles
— Alex (4), Invermere

Making snow angels after a big snowfall
— Angela (3), Jasper